This Journal Belongs To:

Made in the USA
Monee, IL
21 December 2020

55297209R00069